MW00440686

To _____ _Mom_____

From _____ _Ship_____

In appreciation for your positive influence
in the lives of those who look to you for leadership.
May you continue to grow in wisdom and strength
as you learn to lead like Jesus.

On this day__ _27 Oct 2004_____

WORDS
TO LEAD BY

A Practical Daily Devotional
on Leading Like Jesus

Skip Moen, Ph.D.

With Foreword, Comments, and Reflections
by Ken Blanchard and Phil Hodges

insight
PUBLISHING GROUP
Tulsa, Oklahoma

WORDS TO LEAD BY
© 2005 by Skip Moen

Published by Insight Publishing Group
8801 S. Yale, Suite 410
Tulsa, OK 74137
918-493-1718

Unless otherwise noted, Scipture quotations are taken from the New American Standard Bible ®, Copyright © 1960, 1962, 1963, 1968, 1971, 1972, 1973,1975, 1977, 1995 by the Lockman Foundation. Used by permission. Scripture quotations marked NIV are from the New International Version, © 1960, 1962, 1963, 1968, 1971, 1972, 1973, 1975, 1977, 1995 by the Lockman Foundation. Used by permission.

ISBN 1-932503-39-0
Library of Congress catalog card number: 2004112443

Printed in the United States of America

Foreword

Six years ago when we began working with Bill Hybels, Senior Pastor of Willow Creek Community Church near Chicago, on *Leadership by the Book,* we studied Jesus as a leader. We soon realized that everything Ken and Bill wrote or taught about effective leadership over the years, Jesus did. And He did it perfectly. It became clear to all three of us that Jesus was the greatest leadership role model of all time. After all, He mentored twelve ordinary people and with them achieved extraordinary results.

Shortly after this revelation, we decided to start The Center for Faithwalk Leadership—a nonprofit ministry dedicated to challenging and equipping people to lead like Jesus.

One of the blessings of this work has been to read and reread the gospel accounts of how Jesus taught His disciples by word and deed the essence of sacrificial servant leadership. With each reading we became convinced more than ever that in Jesus we have a bottomless well of pure truth about leadership. This became even more evident to us when we met Skip Moen, a gifted scholar and communicator. We were blessed by his insights.

In *Words to Lead By*, Skip shines new light on the meaning and significance of the words Jesus spoke. Skip's knowledge and life experiences led him to become a surrendered servant of the Master with profound insights into His leadership. We are thrilled to be partnering with Skip.

It is our prayer that as you read and reflect on *Words to Lead By*, you will discover new insights and inspiration into how to lead like Jesus and what a privilege it is to follow the One who loves us beyond measure. Come let us follow Him together.

Ken Blanchard and Phil Hodges

Purpose and Process

Leading like Jesus means understanding His beliefs about leadership and putting them into action as your own leadership point of view. The purpose of *Words to Lead By* is to provide you with a deeper understanding of Jesus' leadership beliefs by uncovering the often-overlooked treasure of His words from the ancient texts. As you study and apply the leadership teaching of Jesus in *Words to Lead By*, it is our prayer that your life and influence will be transformed.

There are three parts to the forty daily devotions contained in this book. First will be one of Skip's daily devotions drawn from the words of Jesus as they appear in the Greek Biblical text. Secondly, Comments and Reflections by Ken and Phil follow these devotions. Finally, there is a Personal Insights section for you to record your personal reflections about what you have read and how you intend to put your discovery into action.

We pray that through this process of daily devotions, reflection, and self analysis you will be inspired, challenged, and equipped to let the words of Jesus change your life and your leadership behavior forever.

Skip Moen, Ken Blanchard, and Phil Hodges
Spring 2004

In the Beginning

Leadership begins with this question: Are you willing?

There are many different leadership theories and practices in the market today. Leadership is a hot topic. But biblical leadership does not begin with theory. It begins where Jesus began: in a prayer of submission.

The answer to the most important leadership question, "Are you willing?", will be discovered on your knees. It is a question about your willingness of heart, mind, and soul to submit completely to God's way of leading—as a servant of others.

This short study must begin with your prayer. If you are going to let the words of Jesus mold the kind of leader you will become, you will need to answer, "Yes, Lord. Here I am. Show me how to lead." Until this prayer echoes the desire of your heart, these short studies will be nothing more than words. But when you are ready to lead like Jesus, you will discover that the wisdom of leadership is not hidden from you. It is found in obedience to Him.

This day, _____, I said, "Yes, Lord. I am willing. Reveal to me what it means to lead your way."

Signed: _____

Greatness Guaranteed

*Not so with you. Instead, whoever **wants** to become
great among you must be your servant*
Matthew 20:26 NIV

Wants—What is absolutely guaranteed in life? The joke is that
the only guarantees are death and taxes. But Jesus guarantees
something far better. **He guarantees greatness.**

Jesus will not compromise with "good." He is interested in
great. It's a matter of motivation. He says, "If you are really
determined to become great." Then Jesus tells us that the road
to greatness can be guaranteed. Greatness is certain—if you are
willing to commit yourself to being a servant. Your greatness
does not depend on anything that the world gives or withholds.
It depends only on *determination*.

Jesus was a man of action words. He understood that life
changes require strong commitments. The translation "wants"
is not nearly strong enough to convey what Jesus is saying. It's
not what I *want*. It's what I am *determined to have*.

The Greek verb used here is *thelo*. It is a word that describes
an act of the will. It means to put into action whatever is
needed to accomplish a purpose. People who use this word
aren't wishing on a star. They know that intense desire
requires follow through. This same verb is used many times
to describe the will of God. His purposes *always* are fulfilled
in His actions. That is the kind of movement that Jesus is
looking for. Don't talk the talk if you aren't ready to walk
the walk.

The pathway to greatness is simple. It requires only one
thing—becoming a servant to all. To follow this simple plan

of action will require the biggest commitment you have ever made. But God guarantees the outcome.

Become like the Master—totally committed to serve.

Comments and Reflections:
There is a difference between being interested in doing something and being committed. According to colleague Art Turock, interested people always have an excuse why they can't do what they said they were going to do. Committed people, on the other hand, don't know about excuses. All they know about is results—doing what they said they were going to do no matter what. If you are committed to leading like Jesus, you won't have to do it by yourself. Jesus promises you the Holy Spirit as your guide and day-to-day consultant. A surrendered heart is the first step, followed by commitment. Are you interested or committed to leading like Jesus?

❧❧❧

LETTING THE WORDS OF JESUS CHANGE ME TODAY

How does my life reflect Jesus' challenge to become great?

What did God show me about my personal determination?

What change will I make today as a result of God's leading?

Total Commitment

*His master said to him, 'Well done,
good and faithful **slave**'*
Matthew 25:21

Slave—Not servant! Jesus is not looking for employees.
Jesus addresses His followers as slaves because He wants us
to recognize the necessity of total dependence and complete
submission. A follower of Jesus is not going about his own
business. The "good and faithful slave" is the one whose life
is devoted to fulfilling the tasks given to him by his master.
He waits for orders and then completes them.

In order to lead like Jesus, we will need to first follow like
Jesus. Jesus was devoted completely to the will of His
Father. He is called a *slave* of God. Nothing deterred Him
from fulfilling the task set before Him. If you are going to be
the leader He wants you to be, you must begin by volunteering to be a slave.

In the Greek world this word, *doulos,* means "slave." There
is a big difference between a servant and a slave. It is a
difference that we need to understand and incorporate into
our thinking.

The Greeks treasured freedom. In the Greek mind, freedom
separated men from animals. This demarcation produced a
hierarchy of servants and slaves. Servants were those men
and women who were in the employ of the master. They
may have been indentured for debts but they still were
treated as human beings. But the *doulos* was the slave of the
lowest class. He was nothing more than property. He did
not deserve treatment any better than an animal. His life
was entirely at the whim of the master. He had absolutely
no rights of his own.

Why is this distinction between "servant" and "slave" important? The answer is found in the implication about dependence. A slave was *totally dependent* on the master. He owed everything to his master. He had no means of survival without the master. He had no purpose but to serve the master. The master's will was his life.

Are you a slave of the Master or just an employee?

Comments and Reflections:
Most of us would be more comfortable with the word "servant" rather than "slave" in this passage. That is in fact the word used in many biblical translations. The use of the word "slave" brings the title of one of Bill Hybels' books alive—*Descend Into Greatness*. Unless we are willing to become totally dependent on our Master, we will never reach greatness as a leader.

─── ೲഐ ───

LETTING THE WORDS OF JESUS CHANGE ME TODAY

Have I acted as a "slave" to Jesus or have I been an employee?

What is God showing me about my level of commitment?

What changes need to take place if I am going to be Jesus' slave?

What will I ask in prayer today?

One Day at a Time

*Give us this day our **daily** bread.*
Matthew 6:11

Daily—Today's culture loves entitlement. We all think we deserve things just because we are here. But God has a different view.

This petition in the Lord's Prayer pushes aside any claim that we might have on even the basic necessities of life as our *rights*. Even life's most basic needs are gifts from God. It is not that we are to be content with only the most basic elements of life. Rather, we are to acknowledge that everything, even the bare necessities, come to us as gifts.

The Greek word is *epiousion*. This is one of the most unusual words in the entire Bible. This word appears here in this verse for the first and only time. It is not found in any other biblical context and has no clear cognates in other ancient languages. All of this is even more unusual since the meaning of the word certainly must have been clear to Jesus' disciples and the early Christians. But we can learn something about this word by looking at its parts. *Epi* usually means "upon." *Ousia* is the Greek word for "being" (to exist). Perhaps this word is telling us that God gives us our being—our very existence—one day at a time. Without God's grace, I would simply cease to be. Do you ever thank God that you just are?

We are part of the fellowship of the redeemed. We know that our basic needs must come to us one day at a time. We are healed for this day. We are helped for this day. We are whole for this day. The basic necessities of our lives cannot be stored up for tomorrow nor appropriated from yesterday. We can only live daily. When we say the Lord's Prayer, the word daily has a special significance. This word summarizes our lives. One day at a time.

Do you realize that your leadership is "daily" too? You can lead only one day at a time. Yesterday's efforts are gone. Tomorrow's have not arrived. Today is the only day you can lead.

Comments and Reflections:
Every day we are tempted to be self-serving as leaders rather than serving others. We need to invite God into our lives on a daily basis. Here are two prayers that can help you walk His talk: When you wake up . . . "Lord, I don't know what this day will bring. Please give me the opportunity and help to lead like Jesus." Before going to bed . . . "Lord, I thank you for the opportunity this day to lead like Jesus." Then reflect on the opportunities you had and whether what you did would make Jesus smile. And finally, as you put your head on the pillow, ask the Lord to give you the energy to lead like Jesus when you awaken.

ℬℛ

LETTING THE WORDS OF JESUS CHANGE ME TODAY

Am I the kind of leader who recognizes my daily dependence on God?

How does my daily dependence show itself in the actions of my life?

What am I doing right now to help others see God's daily grace?

What areas of my life need to be placed in the "daily" category?

Be a Waiter!

*It is not so among you, but whoever wishes to
become great among you shall be your **servant***
Matthew 20:26

Servant—What are the characteristics of a great waiter?
First, a great waiter is someone you hardly realize is even
there. A great waiter is someone who makes it possible for
you to enjoy your meal *without* problems or concerns. A
waiter is a background person; someone who makes sure
that the food is hot and delivered on time, that the water
glasses are constantly filled, and that all of your needs are
met. In fact, if you have to call attention to the waiter, it
probably means that something is wrong. A great waiter is
in the business of facilitating life for others.

Jesus was not in the restaurant business, but the metaphor
fits. He was in the "serving others" business. His metaphor
really tells us that there is no place on earth where serving
others is not appropriate. From the top of the ladder to the
bottom, greatness is found in serving others.

The Greek word here is *diakonos*. It is the word we use for
"deacon," but its older meaning was someone who waits on
tables. If you want a mental picture of leading like Jesus,
think of yourself as a waiter.

You don't have to struggle with the question, "What is my
purpose in life?" Jesus has already given you the answer.
God engineers life so that He puts you in exactly the place
He wants you to be at this precise moment in time for the
single purpose of serving others. You can fulfill your
purpose in life every moment of your existence by being a
waiter. Fade into the background. Do what it takes to make

the lives of others better. And the Master will say to you, "Well done."

Comments and Reflections:
To lead like Jesus is to approach every relationship with service in mind. A quick test of your leadership motivation is to reflect on your last attempt at influencing the thinking, behavior, or development of another person and asking yourself: Whose best interest was I seeking to serve?

———————— ෨෬ ————————

LETTING THE WORDS OF JESUS CHANGE ME TODAY

How willing am I to be a waiter on others?

What did I learn about my attitude of a servant?

Who needs me to be their servant today?

First Things First

But seek first His kingdom, and His righteousness;
and all these things shall be added to you.
Matthew 6:33

Seek—You're in the mall with your small child. You turn toward a display window and when you turn back, your child is gone. Instant panic. Immediate, fervent concentration. There is only one thing on your mind. Seeking!

Seeking is a very strong word. It isn't just "looking around" or "checking it out." It is fervent hunting. Every parent knows what this word means. It is the intensity of looking for a lost child. Nothing else matters until that child is found. We are consumed with looking. We will never stop until that child is safe in our arms. We will go to any lengths, use every resource, spend every moment searching until we find what we seek.

Here the word means, "to deliberately strive and desire something as an act of the will." It is the Greek word *zeteo*. The context implies putting your whole life at the disposal of God's rule and will so that nothing takes greater priority. This meaning carries the Old Testament idea that seeking God is an activity of the whole being, not simply an intellectual or religious pursuit. Seeking God is the sacrifice of everything we are for one crucial goal. It is never a part-time occupation or a less than 100 percent effort. *Zeteo* means, "Give it all you've got!"

This verse tells us that whenever we consciously commit ourselves in utter abandonment to God's will, He faithfully cares for our every need. Jesus simply says that God knows exactly what we need and we can have every confidence that He will provide for us when we totally surrender to

Him. This is the essence of life in Christ. We are asked to seek only one thing—God's reign. First things first. Shelter, provision, money, security, companionship are not first on the list. Jesus tells us that the real goal is God's kingdom. We must surrender everything else in order to seek that one essential thing. But when we make God's reign the single focus of life, an amazing thing happens. God takes care of the rest.

When your life is consumed with looking for God, God will find you. And you will be completely cared for. Jesus said it another way. "Blessed are the poor in spirit." It really means, "Happy are the ones who are desperate for God because God will find them."

Comments and Reflections:
Most people measure earthly success in terms of wealth, recognition, power, status, and achievement. There is nothing wrong with acquiring any of these things if they are the outcome of honoring God in all we do. The trouble with these success indicators comes when they become our priority as an expression of our own ego. Then we will never connect with what is most important in God's eyes.

───────────── ෫෬ ─────────────

LETTING THE WORDS OF JESUS CHANGE ME TODAY

What actions in my life clearly reveal my top priorities?

How do my leadership decisions reflect the priority of God's kingdom first?

Would other people recognize my top priority as God's glorification?

It's Not What You Know.
It's What You Do!

*If any man is **willing** to do His will,
he shall know of the teaching, whether it is of God.*
John 7:17

Willing—There is an incredible truth involved in this verse. It is the truth that spiritual knowledge is based on obedience, not on education. Jesus says that we will know the things of God when we do His will. All the study in the world will not make you spiritual. The scribes and Pharisees spent years in study. They understood nothing of God's true intentions. I have hundreds of theology books. I spent decades in school. I have many degrees. None of that made me a more spiritual person. My spirituality depends on only one thing—am I willing?

Our culture believes that education is the solution to our problems. We could stop the spread of AIDS if we just had better educational programs. We could resolve conflicts between countries with better understanding. We could end the Middle East war with clearer objectives. We could save the planet from environmental extinction with more awareness. In the end, none of these efforts will succeed. Why? Because the real issue is not what is happening in my head. It is what is happening in my heart. No change will ever come until I am willing to obey.

Thelo is one of the most important Greek words in the New Testament. It implies more than a conscious thought toward desire. It means to actively carry out the intention. To will is to do.

God knows that talk is cheap. There are no commandments in the Bible that say, "Talk a straight path" or "Think a straight path." The Bible says, "Walk a straight path." Obedience means doing it, right now. If your life is not filled with God's presence, perhaps you have stopped walking. Maybe there is some part of your life that is on vacation from God. If you want to know God, you must first obey. God is ready and waiting to pour His life into yours, to fill you with knowledge of His purposes. But you have to be willing to obey. Walk first.

Comments and Reflections:
The gap between knowing and doing today is much wider than the gap between ignorance and knowledge. More leading like Jesus is the answer; not more knowing about leading like Jesus. Leading like Jesus is a moment-by-moment journey taken one step at a time. It doesn't matter as much where you are in the journey, just starting out or well down the road. What matters is which way you are headed with your next step.

───────────── ଚ୦ଔ ─────────────

LETTING THE WORDS OF JESUS CHANGE ME TODAY

What did God show me about the connection between obedience and knowledge?

Am I leading from obedience or from "knowing what to do"?

What am I doing right now to make obedience the rule of my life?

Day 7

The Essential Imperative

*You shall **love** the Lord your God with all your heart,
and with all your soul, and with all your mind.*
Matthew 22:37

Love—We are so familiar with this verse that we have forgotten just how unusual it is. This verse is really a quotation from Deuteronomy 6:5 where the Hebrew word for "love" is *ahab*. There is nothing unusual about the word itself. It is used for love between a man and a woman, for love of special things, for God's love for His creation, and for man's love for God. What is unusual is that "love" is commanded.

Reflect on this for a moment. We live in a world that views love as an uncontrollable emotion. We "fall" in love. It overpowers us. From this perspective, it is quite impossible to tell someone that they must "love" another person. If love were based on feelings and emotions, such a command would be ridiculous. I could no more force myself to alter my emotions toward another person than I could make myself enjoy the taste of sour milk. Yet God commands us to love Him. Clearly, the biblical view of love is not about "never having to say you're sorry."

The Greek word used to translate this quotation from Hebrew is *agapeseis*. It is an active, present tense imperative. Do this right now! This Greek word was in very little use before the New Testament writers adopted it for their purposes. They gave it a meaning that clearly distinguishes this word for love and the Greek idea of love as personal desire. *Agape* love is the love of self-sacrifice. It is the paradigm of the servant leader. In this usage, it is not about my feelings, it is about my actions. Jesus was often frustrated with the development of His followers. He was angry at the hypocrisy of the Pharisees. He was distraught over the unrepentant behavior of Israel. But none of those feelings changed His commitment to obedience, sacrifice, and action. *Agape* love can be commanded because it is about choices I make, commitments I live by, and directions I take from God.

Once I heard a man say, "Oh, I love God but I just can't get along with those people. I can't help it. It's just how I feel." He didn't understand a thing about *agape*. The love of a follower of Jesus does not depend on how I feel but on what I do. God says, "Act with self-sacrifice in every part of your life. Then you will be loving me because you will be reflecting how I act toward you."

Comments and Reflections:
Learning to lead like Jesus has one nonnegotiable requirement: to actively express the love of God beyond sentimentality and emotion in your interactions with others. Here is a growth giving challenge—identify an individual or group of people you have trouble loving. Following God's commandment, how can you behave differently towards these people even if you don't change your attitude towards them?

ജ

LETTING THE WORDS OF JESUS CHANGE ME TODAY

How does my life demonstrate love as a decision, not an emotion?

Who do I need to "love" as an active decision?

What do I need to do to make this active decision become a reality in my life?

Just One Condition

This is My commandment, that you love one another,
***just as** I have loved you.*
John 15:12

Just as—The love commandment of Jesus is *conditional*. It is
not like the great commandment to love God with all your
heart, mind, and strength. Jesus adds a qualifier, the Greek
word *kathos*. He doesn't say, "Love one another." He says,
"Love just as I loved." Jesus does not expect you to do
anything more than what He has done. His commandment
is *conditioned* by the example of His own life.

Kathos is a combination word. It is made up of *kata*,
"according to" and *hos*, "in the same manner." If we are to
understand Jesus' *conditional commandment*, we need to
know what *hos* means. In classical Greek, the translation
would be "just as." But within the umbrella of this small
word is an entire theology. *Hos* implies a manner of
complete likeness. It means, "the equivalent of." It takes on
the sense of "demonstrating the same quality." It can mean,
"belonging to the same essence or substance."

What a relief! Reading this verse I might think that I was
expected to love everyone like God loves everyone. But now we
see that Jesus isn't asking that at all. He is just asking that I love
others in the same manner and with exactly the essence that He
loved me. So, all I have to do is what He did—be totally
committed to the Father's purpose and be completely willing to
lay down my life for those who hate me. Wasn't that easy!

It is ironic that we spend so much time focused on the first
part of this verse and forget the fact that Jesus calls us to just
be like He is. That's all. Just do what Jesus would do. I don't
have to search the heavens for insight or instruction about

loving others. All I have to do is read about Him. See how simple it is! To be like Him. Clear. Direct. More than enough. If we thought that Jesus relaxed His commandment with this condition, we need to think again. This kind of condition is more unconditional than ever. Leading like Jesus has only one condition—love others like He did.

Comments and Reflections:
Loving others, especially the people who look to you for leadership, as Jesus loves you means providing sacrificial service of their best interests. It can take many forms, including guiding them beyond their current level of development and understanding, requiring both forgiveness and patience. Think about where you would be if the love you received depended on your performance.

ଽଔ

LETTING THE WORDS OF JESUS CHANGE ME TODAY

How does my life reflect the condition of Jesus' love command?

What acts of sacrificial love I have made toward others?

Do others see me as a reflection of Jesus' love sacrifice?

Modeling the Master

*. . . for whatever the Father does, these things the
Son also does **in like manner**.*
John 5:19

In like manner—In this verse we see that Jesus does
nothing except what the Father does, and what He does is
an exact copy of the Father's will and purposes. Jesus is the
fully dependent man! He does not exercise His own plans,
praying, "Father help me to complete my goals." He does
only what the Father desires. "Father, help me to do your
purposes, not mine."

Forget the miracles for a moment. Think about all of the
other actions of Jesus. The tender care, the teaching, the
coaching, the prayer, the discussions, the interactions—all
of it, says Jesus, is a reflection of the Father's actions. Is it
any wonder that Jesus could tell the disciples, "If you have
seen me, you have seen the Father"? Too often we think
only of the spectacular signs as the work of the Father
through the Son. But Jesus corrects this misunderstanding.
Walking to Nazareth is the Father's will. Eating at the
wedding is the Father's will. Praying on the mountaintop is
the Father's will. Sleeping in the boat is the Father's will.
"Do all to the glory of God," says Paul. He is simply
pointing to the way that Jesus lived.

The Greek word *homoios* comes from a word group that
defines the idea of being the same. The general sense of
these words is "an exact duplication or copy" or "of the
same kind." God intends that all of His children will take on
the same character as His only Son. God's purpose is to
make us *like* His Son. That means we will not do anything
unless it reflects the Father's will. Is that the way you are
living today?

Comments and Reflections:
If you lead like Jesus, every action will express what the Father wills. It is not the "big" things that count. It is the moment-by-moment everyday habits and patterns that make someone a servant leader. Think of something you do every day that you can turn into a new expression of worship and gratitude.

፠ৎ৩

LETTING THE WORDS OF JESUS CHANGE ME TODAY

Am I the kind of leader who duplicates the character of Jesus?

How do my actions show others that I serve the perfect Master?

Am I aware that God is active in every decision of my life?

What daily little thing can I turn into a celebration of God's will for me?

Lifting the Load

*And they tie up **heavy loads**, and lay them on men's shoulders; but they themselves are unwilling to move them with so much as a finger.*
Matthew 23:4

Heavy loads—Shipping freight. Massive cargo. Take a trip to the docks. Watch those gigantic cranes lifting roll-on trailers. Now imagine it all on your back. It's a weight none of us can bear. The Greek combination *phortia barea* means just that.

But Jesus is not talking about the weight of sin. He is talking about the weight of religious and cultural rules. We could just as easily add the weight of all the expectations put on our own lives. As servant leaders, our job is to lift those burdens from others—to free others for the service God called them to do, not the slavery men place upon them. If you are following in His footsteps, your reaction to oppressed people will be the same as His—"Come to me and I will give you rest."

Jesus observed that those who were preoccupied with rules and rituals were most often the ones who gladly shifted burdens onto others but who routinely avoided taking any responsibility on themselves. How many of us have gone through that experience? Seeing the boss becomes traumatic because it means that the workload just got bigger. What a difference it would make if the boss came to us and said, "How can I help lift the load you are carrying today?"

We all have the option of being a taskmaster or a servant leader. It really doesn't matter if you are at home, school, or work. You can always dump another burden on someone if you wish. Or you can take another approach. You can become a servant leader like Jesus.

Jesus led by lifting. He made lifting a principle of living in order to take the burden from our shoulders. Being a servant means carrying the freight for someone else.

Comments and Reflections:
The 80/20 principle of goal setting suggests that focusing on a few things—the 20 percent—can give you 80 percent of the desired results. Lightening the load for your people doesn't mean doing their work for them. It means helping them sort out where they need to focus their attention, clearing away barriers to their performance, praising progress, redirecting them when they are headed in the wrong direction, practicing patience, and helping them to succeed.

⁊⁊⁊

LETTING THE WORDS OF JESUS CHANGE ME TODAY

Would others see me as a leader who lifts away burdens or as a leader who demands that others do more?

What actions can I take right now to lift the burden of someone I know?

How am I being a servant who carries the burdens of those God has placed in my sphere of influence?

Where do I need God to help me become a better freight handler?

Take It! It's Yours.

*. . . whoever does not **receive** the kingdom of
God like a child shall not enter it at all.*
Mark 10:15

Receive—Offer a gift to a child. Hold the present in your hand
and watch what happens. If your children are like mine, you
will hardly be able to hold them back. They will rush to grab
the present. The wrapping will fly off with shouts of joy. They
will be entirely focused on just one thing—to make that
present their own.

Sometimes nuances make a big difference. There is a slight
shade of difference between "receive" and "take." It is this
difference that matters here. The Greek verb *dechomai* is in
the middle voice, a form that implies something of special
significance to the subject. So the real sense of this statement
from the Master is "whoever does not take." It is a statement
of deliberate choice and active decision. If you are going to
enter into God's kingdom, you need to be like a child in
front of a present. You need to *take* this gift for yourself. It
will not be yours through passive acknowledgement. No
one is going to walk over to you and place it in your unmo-
tivated hands. Be like a child. Take it!

We have a saying that reflects some of this attitude. "Grab
life by the horns." Get involved. Don't sit on the sidelines
waiting for something to happen. Get up and dance. Jesus
saw this same open exuberance in children. They were
active participants in the joyful celebration of living. Even
though they were completely dependent on the watchful
care of their parents, they never acted with concern or
worry. Dependence was the reality that allowed them to
live without care.

God offers an incredible gift to each of us. Jesus says, "Jump up and take it. Make it yours. Claim it for yourself. Be like a child. Stop worrying about the cost/benefit ratio, the liability issues, the legal responsibilities, or the social protocol. Take the gift!"

Every leader offers a gift to every follower. But it is only a gift. It cannot become a possession until it is taken from the leader and made my own.

Comments and Reflections:
Leading like Jesus is a give and take process. A leader must be willing to surrender control and the follower must receive it and accept accountability to use it as it was intended. There are bound to be times in your leadership efforts when you are willing to give up control but those you are attempting to lead are unwilling or unable to receive it. A servant leader walks a fine line between taking the blame for delegating prematurely and holding people accountable.

❧❧

LETTING THE WORDS OF JESUS CHANGE ME TODAY

How would I describe my emotions about God's gift offered to me?

Am I a leader who eagerly anticipates God's interaction with me?

What do I do to offer the gifts God has given me to others?

Which Way Is Up?

*For everyone who **exalts** himself shall be humbled,*
*and he who **humbles** himself shall be exalted.*
Luke 14:11

Exalts—Humbles—in our world, the top floor office, the reserved parking space, the private jet, and the chauffeured car measure success. Many times I have heard the expression, "making it to the top." But God's view turns the world on its head. If you want success in His kingdom, seek the basement.

How many executives do you know who don't have a reserved parking spot? How many do you know who don't take the largest corner office? How many CEO's do you know who lead from the basement? If the penthouse is your plan, you have probably missed being a servant leader.

These two words are the buttons in God's elevator: *hupsoo* meaning, "to go up to the top" and *tapeinos* meaning, "to go down to the bottom." Do you want to live in God's penthouse? Then take the elevator to the basement. You see, in God's world you need to live below the ground floor in order to fulfill the purposes of serving others. In fact, the Greek word for "bearing another's burden" is a word that comes from the construction trade. It's like getting down in the dirt and lifting up the foundation on your shoulders. In God's world, the penthouse is downstairs. Jesus is using words that give us a very vivid picture of truth. It's a matter of up and down.

Jesus was exalted—after volunteering to give up divinity. Jesus was lifted up—after going down to the grave. Jesus was honored—after submitting to the Father. Jesus was glorified—after dying. Exalting God only is the DOWN button on the ego elevator. Ego deflation is the pathway of a man after God's heart.

Comments and Reflections:
As you reflect on your own story, it might be useful to ask yourself which floor you choose when the elevator doors close.

───────────── ⁊ↄᏩ ─────────────

LETTING THE WORDS OF JESUS CHANGE ME TODAY

What am I doing today to keep EGO down?

Who have I invited to act as my EGO check partner?

Is my goal to serve from below or from the top?

What does God have on my prayer agenda about this?

Let It Be

*But Jesus answering said to him, "**Permit** it at this time"*
Matthew 3:15

Permit—How often have we been confronted by this simple request? "Just do what I ask," says Jesus. And we hesitate. "No, Lord. It doesn't seem right to me. You must be mistaken." But, of course, He isn't. He knows exactly what He is asking. So He reminds us, "Just let it be." The first recorded word spoken by Jesus sets the stage for His entire ministry. It is the right word for us when we begin to follow Jesus.

Let's paint the picture of this story and see how this applies.

John sees Jesus coming to him to be baptized. John protests. "No, Lord. You should be baptizing me." But Jesus says, "John, it's OK. *Let it be.*" Send away your concern, John. Release yourself to my desire. I know what is needed. Just do what I ask.

In Greek, the word is *aphes*. It is from a verb that combines *apo* (from) and *hiemi* (to send), "to send from" or "to send away." It has the sense of leaving things as they are.

Jesus wrote the original score for Paul McCartney's hit *Let It Be*. He knew that there is a divine order that must prevail. He came to John in humility and asked John to just do what He wanted to be done.

"Don't worry, John. I know what is necessary. God is in control here. Just do what I ask."

You can start with John in the water of the Jordan. Jesus comes to you and to me. He says only one thing: Just do what I ask. Let the rest go.

Will you be able to do what John did? Standing before John was the Son of Man. John understood and obeyed. Let it be. John took Jesus in his arms and fulfilled Jesus' desire. That is all we need to do. Let the rest go.

Comments and Reflections:
Before you can hope to lead like Jesus, you have to be willing to surrender control. To be a servant leader like Jesus you have to let go and let God. A question we need to ask ourselves on a regular basis is: Am I willing to let go and let God and if not—why not?

───────── ଛଔ ─────────

LETTING THE WORDS OF JESUS CHANGE ME TODAY

How easily do I accept Jesus' requests?

What is Jesus asking me to "allow" Him to do in my life today?

If I agree to His requests, what will change for me today?

Wait a Moment

Father, if Thou art willing, remove this cup from
*Me; yet not My will, **but** Thine be done.*
Luke 22:42

But—The life of a servant leader is built around a pause. It is the pause that separates short-term results from the long-term effectiveness. Jesus faced exactly the same pause. He saw a shorter way *but* He chose the more effective route.

The Greek word *alla* is a very strong word. It does not mean "slightly different" or "a modification." It means "antithesis," opposite and emphatic contrast. It is the "night and day" word. It is the word we would use when we come to a cross-road. Only one way is the effective, long-range path. The other way is quick results at the expense of submission and obedience. When a servant leader confronts a crossroad decision, there must be a pause built into life.

If we think that Jesus had it all mapped out for Him, we are mistaken. Here we see Jesus at the moment of greatest challenge—and greatest temptation. The shorter way stood open to Him. But obedience required a longer road. Jesus sees that the path ahead will be hard. It will be full of scorn, suffering, and rejection. But He also knows that His purpose in life is to follow the Father's will *no matter what the cost*. This is the only way of true discipleship. So Jesus pauses. *Alla*—but. But not what I choose. But not what might seem easier for me. But not what I want. It is the Father's direction that must be followed. Jesus spoke the most important words ever spoken, "not my will but yours."

Abba, Father, let me make *alla* the turning point in my choices. Not the short way, but the right way, no matter what the cost. Let every decision begin with a pause.

Comments and Reflections:
The power to lead like Jesus will flow only when we choose His will above our own. It's our pride and fear that edges God out and seeks our own way. We must pause and recalibrate our commitment to "His will not ours" on a daily basis through solitude, prayer, and study of His Holy words in Scripture.

ഇരു

LETTING THE WORDS OF JESUS CHANGE ME TODAY

What did I discover about the need for a pause in my own efforts to influence others?

How do my actions demonstrate my understanding of the divine pause?

Where do I need to build in a pause in my life?

The Reason Why

*For **this** I have been born, and for **this** I have come
into the world, to bear witness to the truth.*
John 18:37

This—Most of us have no idea why we are born. We spent
our lives in search of purpose. And life does not give up its
answers easily. We often discover that what we thought was
our purpose in life is suddenly replaced by something else.
We are unfocused creatures.

But not Jesus. He knew absolutely what His life was all
about. And nothing deterred Him from completing His
purpose. He came to die. The next time you read the story
of the last week of His life, take notice about who is in
charge of the events. Too often we think that the forces of
evil pushed these circumstances onto the pages of history.
But that is not so. Jesus Himself was the active agent. He
chose the timing. He chose the situation. He initiated,
pushed, and propelled the actions that led to the cross. Jesus
knew why He was born.

Touto is the Greek pronoun for *this*. It is an ordinary
pronoun. There is nothing spectacular about it. Except here.
Here Jesus says that His entire reason for being is *this*—to
give testimony to the truth. Jesus understood with absolute
clarity that He was born to die. His purpose for living was
dying. He lived His life with this objective constantly in
mind. He knew where He was going.

No one of us can choose when we are born, but every one of
us can choose when we will die. We can choose to **die now**
by identifying ourselves with the death of Christ and giving
up our old lives, or we can try to postpone death by

avoiding the call of God. That means we will **die later** at a time of His choosing.

Only the Christ could choose when to be born. But we are like Him in this: we can choose when to die. We can take part in the purpose of life by choosing to echo His words, "For this I have been born." We can die to ourselves in order to be born from above in Him.

Comments and Reflections:
Enter each day with anticipation. It contains a moment God has been planning to express His purpose for creating you. A moment that He has planned since before time began to express His grace and mercy through you. Entering your day with the same trusting anticipation as a child asking a parent, "Where are we going today and what are we going to do?" will let God be the Lord of your day and your work.

                              ഹരുഃ

LETTING THE WORDS OF JESUS CHANGE ME TODAY

What is the mission statement for my life?

How does my identification with His death change how I will act today?

What was I born to do in God's kingdom?

Protective Custody

*While I was with them, I was **keeping** them in Thy name*
John 17:12

Keeping—Jesus was the warden. This Greek word, *eteroun*, comes from the arena of jails. It means, "to act as a guard over a prison, to keep an eye on someone, to be a warden." But not everyone in a prison is there because they are evil. Sometimes we put people into "protective custody." That is exactly what God did. God gave His Son the keys to the kingdom. Some of those keys were designed to lock people inside in order to protect them. In the great priestly prayer of John 17, Jesus is reporting that while He was on watch, He protected those who were entrusted into His care. He locked them away from the enemy and from evil forces that sought to destroy them. In the end, Jesus fulfilled this role for all of us with His death. Hebrews tells us that He overcame the enemy that kept us captive all of our lives. He never left His post and He never gave up the keys.

Every servant leader has guard duty. Protection is part of the assignment. A leader who does not protect the people under his care is nothing more than a tyrant. The world today is full of examples of people who thought of themselves as leaders but who failed in every respect to guard those under their care. Many of today's leaders have shown that ego was their guide. They lived the motto, "What's yours is mine." They forgot that they were responsible for protective custody.

Servant leaders take this responsibility seriously. They follow the Master. He laid down His life to protect His own. Look at the verse once again. Jesus specifically says that His guard duty was an assignment from God and that He completed it under God's authority. He kept them in God's name. This is the thought of a servant leader. There are no accidents in life. God gives others into our care so that we may guard them. Every person we influence is part of the group assigned to our protective custody. It is a task handed down from the One who cared for us.

Comments and Reflections:
Having guard duty doesn't mean you don't hold people accountable for their behavior. But it does mean you don't let other people take pot shots at your people without coming to their defense. While you need to hold people accountable for their behavior, it is important that they realize you are on their side and mean them no harm. One way that people know if they can trust you is how you handle their reputations when challenged by others.

80CR

LETTING THE WORDS OF JESUS CHANGE ME TODAY

Does my life show the sacrifices of a guardian of others?

What am I doing now to protect those in my care?

What help do I need from God to fulfill my responsibilities of protective custody?

By Invitation Only

*And He said, "**Come!**" And Peter got out*
of the boat, and walked on the water
Matthew 14:29

Come—You can't receive an RSVP unless you give an invitation.

We might think that this is just a common command. "Come to me!" It seems ordinary enough until we reflect a little on the multifaceted use of this Greek word in the New Testament. More than any other single verb, this action expresses the entire ministry of Jesus.

The Greek word is *erchomai*. It describes the ordinary activity of motion. But it also has a special religious meaning, namely, an approach toward God. We find this in the Old Testament references about coming to the house of the Lord. This nuance of the word is expanded significantly with the coming of Jesus. Jesus' ministry is seen in various applications of this word. He comes to ransom many. He comes to set new life in order. He comes to seek the lost. He asserts over and over that the Kingdom of God has come. He warns of the coming judgment. He comes to His own but they reject Him. He invites all those who hear to "come unto me." Every facet of His leadership is incorporated in some sense of the word "come." It is God's offer to mankind.

The most important thought behind this word is that of invitation. It is not an announcement about new rules and regulations. It is not a notice of what is expected. Jesus did not say, "Make it happen" or "Earn your way." He was not a "what have you done for me lately" leader. He invited men to respond to His purposes and He provided them all of the coaching and instruction needed to do so. If we are to serve as followers of the Lord, our lives must also reflect this invitation. This is more than "open door" policies. The servant leader does not sit behind the desk and wait for someone to approach him. He goes out and invites them. Do not be afraid. Come to me, and I will help.

Comments and Reflections:
To lead like Jesus, your people have to know that you are there for them—ready to help. Is your door open to them? Or do they think they have to fight through barriers to get your ear? Have you given out your invitations today for your people to come to you if they need help? If not, why not? If yes, what are you doing to make them feel welcome if they come?

                                         ഹരു

LETTING THE WORDS OF JESUS CHANGE ME TODAY

What am I doing to invite others to come to me for help?

Does my invitation include all those God brings across my path?

What is God showing me about my willingness to be open to someone else's need?

Possible Perfection

*Therefore you are to be **perfect**, as your heavenly Father is **perfect**.*
Matthew 5:48

Perfect—Oh, the clarity of the goal! Be perfect. But how onerous it seems if we do not understand the Greek. "Perfect" is the English translation of the word *teleios*. But the Greek sense of this word is not the same as our usual English understanding. We think of perfect with an almost mathematical frame of reference. "Without defect" or "without mistake." This is a negative definition. It tells us what is *not* the case. And it is entirely impossible. Can you think of a single real object in the universe that is without any defects? Our mathematical model of reality steers us in the wrong direction because the real meaning of this Greek word is organic, not mathematically static. It really means, "to be fully complete, to be grown up, to have reached its goal or purpose."

What a difference! Can I ever be without a single defect (mathematically perfect)? No. But can I reach the goal of my intended purpose; can I be all that God wants me to be? Yes, again I say, YES! That is my goal. To be fully complete in Him. To be just like Him. To be all that He wants me to be. God promises that He will complete me. He will make sure that all that is necessary for my completion is accomplished.

If "perfect" meant "without a single defect," it would be the impossible goal of being God. God is the only being who is without defect. But God is also the Being who is all that He should be. He is completely fulfilled in His purposes. And that is what He wants for me. God wants me to become the destiny that He purposes me to be. My goal is to be all that

I can be, and He endorses that goal wholeheartedly. He wants me to be everything I was designed to be.

Be perfect! Grow up and become the fulfillment of His destiny for you. Be completely what He wants. It's the clearest goal in the universe. Become what you were designed to be.

Comments and Reflections:
As you pursue the perfection of surrender in serving God's purpose for your leadership, praise progress in even the smallest victories over pride and fear. God is sure to notice.

ഇരു

LETTING THE WORDS OF JESUS CHANGE ME TODAY

Does my leadership goal reflect progress or perfection?

Where do I need progress today?

What am I doing to praise the progress of others?

20/20 Vision

*It was neither that this man sinned, nor his parents; but it was in order that the works of God might be **displayed** in him.*
John 9:3

Displayed—Who is blind in this story? It isn't the man at the side of the road. It is the disciples of Jesus. The disciples saw only the pitiful condition of the man born blind. They did not see what Jesus saw. God put this blind man in their pathway in order that this blind man might minister to them. The disciples asked about the cause of his blindness. They wanted to blame someone. But Jesus saw the *purpose*. The purpose of this blind man was to give those who had eyes the ability to see.

The Greek word here is *phaneroo*. It means, "to make apparent, visible, or known." It is the perfect word for the blindness of the disciples. They had sight but they could not see. Jesus revealed to them a truth much deeper than the issue of blame. He led them to open their eyes to the opportunity of God.

A servant leader must have eyes that "see" the opportunities to reveal God's glory. Many times those opportunities present themselves in unexpected ways. A blind man does not appear to be a likely candidate to demonstrate sight. But God is not limited by human conditions. We are blind only if we do not see who He is.

We have two choices here. We can see what the disciples saw. Problems, impossibilities, blame, despair, and sin. Or we can see what Jesus saw. God at work!

Having eyes that receive images makes no difference at all unless we know what we are seeing. The servant leader is constantly looking for an opportunity from God. A problem is a potential victory. The impossible is divinely routine. Despair is the doorway to hope. Sin is the schoolteacher of forgiveness. Blame is the backhand of purpose. "It all depends on how you look at it."

What do you see?

Comments and Reflections:
Earlier we mentioned that a major challenge of leading like Jesus is the intimacy it requires. In addition to staying in intimate contact with Jesus, leadership requires developing an openness and willingness to see and respond to the individual skills, levels of development needs, and aspirations of your people.

A prayer for each day is to ask God for spiritual eyesight to see people and situations from His point of view. Improving your eyesight comes with a responsibility to respond in a new way to what you see.

⸂⸃

LETTING THE WORDS OF JESUS CHANGE ME TODAY

Am I open to the unexpected intersections of God in my life?

Am I focused on blame or on purpose?

What do I need to ask God today about my spiritual eyesight?

Counting the Cost

For which one of you, when he wants to build a tower,
does not first sit down and **calculate** *the cost*
Luke 14:28

Calculate—What does a pebble have to do with building a tower? Jesus uses a Greek word, *psephizei,* that came from the marketplace. It was a small stone used like the beads in an abacus. A way to keep track of the addition. If you didn't get the pebbles right, your great big tower would never be finished. Unless you were careful with the smallest pebbles, all those giant rocks would amount to nothing.

This is another picture of the life of a servant. "You have been faithful over little, now I will make you steward over much." You counted the pebbles, now I will let you build the tower. Life's accomplishments do not begin with boulders. They begin with pebbles. If you are going to *lead like Jesus,* you must first get all your pebbles in order.

How many of us rush to complete the project only to discover that some tiny detail that was overlooked means the whole effort is lost? Business legend is full of such stories. From NASA to baby cribs, one missing tiny detail has led to disastrous results. Everyone knows the General Motors story of the Nova imported to South America. Product marketing forgot that "Nova" sounds like *no va,* which means "doesn't go" in Spanish. The car was a complete flop because of a word. Pebbles before boulders.

Jesus tells us that unless we count pebbles, the project of life-building for God will never be completed. But when we count the cost, we will discover that no matter how many pebbles we have, it will not be enough. In this project, we must have the stone of the corner, the rock of salvation.

There is only one place to find such a stone. It is not free, but it has been paid for.

Comments and Reflections:
Jesus never misrepresented or minimized the cost of following Him and He never misrepresented the reward. Leading like Jesus means being committed to truth telling and compassionate realism. Trust is built not on overstating the good news and hiding the bad but on confidence in the integrity of the news giver.

─── ∞ ───

LETTING THE WORDS OF JESUS CHANGE ME TODAY

How do my life choices reflect "counting the cost" of following Jesus?

Am I committed to facing the truth no matter what the cost?

How does my leadership influence demonstrate total commitment to the truth?

Relocation Policy

*. . . and everyone who lives and believes **in** Me shall never die.*
John 11:26

In—The Kingdom of Heaven has a relocation plan. Today
the Greek word is *eis*. You probably expected to look at the
word "lives" or "believes." But the preposition is so important that it cannot be passed over. The translation in this
verse is not a good one. The preposition *eis* is really about
"place." It has the sense of "into," like "he went *into* the
house" or "I moved *into* a new position." Why is this so
important? Because the entire gospel of John teaches us that
believing is an activity that moves us from one place to
another. It is not about intellectual assent to certain facts.
That would be, "I believe *in* Christ"—that is, I believe the
facts about this man. No, John says that believing is an
action of the will. It moves me from a world dominated by
moral activity based on my self *into* a world where my
moral activity is based on the character and demands of
Jesus. *Eis* tells me that I must be taken *out* of one place and
put *into* another place. That is what faith is—it is movement
of my whole being out of myself and *into* Christ. It is heavenly relocation.

John uses the word "believe" ninety-two times in his gospel.
Never once is it a noun. It is always a verb—an action of
motion from one state to another. No one can be a follower
of Jesus without moving from self to Christ, says John. No
one can just "sign on the dotted line." "Believing into"
means action.

Jesus says, "The person who has been moved from the place
of serving self *into* the place of serving Me, the person who
has been transferred from his world *into* My world—will do
amazing things." Do you get the sense of this? You must

stand in the world owned and operated by Christ if you are going to do these things. You must be moved out of yourself, away from what you were, and *into* His world, under His control before you have "belief." It's not church, prayers, membership, choir, offerings, or being a better person. It's total relocation. It's pulling up stakes in one world and moving to another. You can't leave some of you behind. You are either in *His* place or you are in some other place. And in His place, you live by His rules, His control, and His direction. His place is FANTASTIC! AMAZING! INCREDIBLE!

Eis, that tiny word, says that I have been transported from death into life. *Into* Christ. There is nowhere else I want to be. Relocation never felt so good!

Comments and Reflections:
Sometimes we get so caught up in the flow of the moment that we lose sight of how far we have come. Think about what your life and leadership was like before you came into Christ and how it is now. Thank God for the difference.

— ✠ —

LETTING THE WORDS OF JESUS CHANGE ME TODAY

How does my life demonstrate my "relocation" to God's Kingdom?

What areas of my life need to be given to God for total relocation?

Remaining Under

*But the one who **endures** to the end, he shall be saved.*
Matthew 24:13

Endures—Do you like secrets? Here is a secret, hidden in this Greek word. It is the secret of revealing Christ in a culture that does not acknowledge Him. This Greek word is *hupomeno*. It literally means, "to remain beneath." What is the method of a servant leader? Here it is, in this word—remain under. Take the DOWN staircase. Lift from below. Keep ego out.

Meno, however, means more than "stay the course." It is also used to describe, "abide, live, and dwell." It is a word that describes our very being. Jesus used it in some critical passages ("Abide in me"). Paul employed the word when he described God's view of love (I Cor. 13:7). It isn't just stoic resignation putting up with the anti-Christian culture. It is a word of active engagement, a word about how we breathe, move, respond, and react. It is about living as a servant. Jesus promises that "remaining under" will produce salvation.

There is one other secret here. This verb is a completed action in the past. The emphasis of this verse is not on the person but on the action. It's not about me. It's "remaining under" that matters. Do you see that this action continues to the end? That word is *telos* from the same word translated in English as "perfect" in Matthew 6:48. It means, "fully complete, grown." "Remain under until your completion," says Jesus.

Winston Churchill is famous for the statement, "Never, never, never, never give up." Jesus said that same thing two thousand years earlier. Be the one who remains under until completion. Live your life in the basement and God will give you the keys to heaven.

Comments and Reflections:
Leading like Jesus means remaining a "work in progress" under the guidance of the Holy Spirit. The work will progress only when you stay in the role of a servant. It means finding joy in doing whatever the work is in front of you because your walking with your Lord.

— ઍଠ —

LETTING THE WORDS OF JESUS CHANGE ME TODAY

What am I doing now that keeps me open to the Holy Spirit's guidance?

What changes do others recognize in me?

How does the realization that I am a work in progress change the way I lead others?

Emotional Management

*Why are you timid, **you men of little faith?***
Matthew 8:26

You men of little faith—I have a nickname. So do many others. Jesus often gave nicknames to His followers. Jesus is literally giving His disciples as a group a nickname, "small convictions." All of this in one word. The Greek word for this entire phrase is *oligopistoi*. It is the combination of two Greek words, *oligos* (meaning "small") and *pistis* (meaning "conviction").

What a joke! Jesus must have had a good laugh. Just consider how funny this situation really is. Jesus and the disciples are in a boat on the sea. Jesus is asleep. A storm comes and the disciples anticipate the worst. Here are men who are in the presence of God and they are afraid of drowning. They wake Him up and plead for help. Do you see the humor in this? The very God who created everything and who controls everything is right there with them and yet they are worried for their lives. Jesus points out how ridiculous they are being by making a joke of their fears. He probably laughed to Himself when He said it.

Did you notice another important element of this statement? Jesus does not belittle or reprimand them. He does not say, "You're so stupid to be worried." He just makes a joke. He lightens the mood. He moves the focus from the circumstances to the attitude. He recognizes immediately that these men have a lot to learn about Him and His purposes, and He begins to teach them by changing the emotions of the situation.

The servant leader sees the depth of the situation, but that depth is not always what must be communicated. In order for truth to be fully assimilated, emotional resistance must be overcome. Followers cannot hear what the leader has to say if they are focused on some other pressing matter. First, a change in emotion. Then a look in the right direction. Leadership begins with understanding the mind-set of the followers.

How often have we tried to lead by forcing our view on others? How often have we failed to hear the worries others have before we began to override their concerns? How many times have we neglected to understand the emotions that prevent the truth from being accepted? It doesn't matter if you are absolutely right. Fear blocks truth. Deal with the fear first.

Comments and Reflections:
Leading like Jesus means loving and leading people beyond their fears. Think back to a time when you dealt successfully with the fears of your people and the impact on their performance. Carry this memory forward as an encouragement during future tests of faith in your leadership.

—— ✺ ——

LETTING THE WORDS OF JESUS CHANGE ME TODAY

How well do I do at managing my emotions?

What steps do I take to address the emotions of my group before I look at goals?

What do I do to help others overcome fear?

Fill in the Blank

Why is it that you were looking for me?
*Did you not know that I had to be in My father's **house**?*
Luke 2:49

House—This verse is about the *scope* of our commitment. Do we have a *spiritual* part of life and a separate *business* part of life? Does Jesus give you advice on your P&L? Does He interview your new hires? Is He there at the planning table?

The word "house" in this verse is not really there at all. By inserting it, we might get the idea that there is part of life that is God's and part that is ours. What a mistake! Literally, the Greek says, "I must be *in My Father's these*." It is a very unusual sentence. We add other words to make sense of it in English. But perhaps we are too anxious to fill in the gaps. Perhaps what Jesus is saying is considerably deeper than we imagine a twelve year old might say.

If we take this statement of Jesus and fill in the gap, we will be led in the direction of seeing His commitment as "part" of His life, the part that He committed to His Father's house or His Father's affairs. But what if we read the verse as it is? What if we recognize that it is a statement about existence, not a statement about partitions? The meaning of this odd Greek construction must be supplied from the context. That is exactly how we should look at our own servant leader lives. We need to let God supply the meaning to our lives from the context.

There are no partitions of involvement in the life of a servant leader. There is only "my Father's these." All of who I am is about what God wants. The context of my life supplies the meaning. In this study, we have seen that "It's not about you." We recognized that Jesus says, "It's about us." We understand now that it's about abiding under Him and under the others we serve. We know that it's about everything we have, everything we are, and everything we hope to be. We know that it's about perfect completion of His purposes. And now we see that it's about context. What is the context of your life? Is it all about God?

Comments and Reflections:
As you lead others, are you being about the "these" of your Father?

───────── ℘℃ℛ ─────────

LETTING THE WORDS OF JESUS CHANGE ME TODAY

How do my actions show that God sets the context for ALL my life?

What am I doing to allow God to shape the context of my life today?

What do I need to pray about now?

Your Leadership Blood Line

*. . . unless one is **born** again, he cannot see the kingdom of God.*
John 3:3

Born—This is a verse about your birth certificate. But it only asks one question. Who is your Father?

Our usual image of birth is associated with the mother, not the father. But in this verse, the verb focuses our attention on conception, not the moment of birth delivery. In Jesus thought, we are "born" when we are conceived. Nicodemus understood perfectly. He does not ask how a man can be "birthed" again. He asks how a man can return to the pre-conception stage and be "generated" again. Both Jesus and Nicodemus are talking about the role of the father. The difference is that Jesus has a somewhat different Father in mind.

Jesus' point is that it is the father's participation that determines the family line in a birth. The Greek verb here is *gennao*. If you sound it out, you will discover the sound of the English word "generate." Here this verb describes the *male* parent's participation in life. Of course, physically the female carries the child during gestation. But Jesus is interested in the conceptual part of the birth process. He wants us to see that at the moment of conception the stamp of family lineage is determined. The child that results is in the *father's* family forever.

Jesus sweeps away everything that Nicodemus stood for. In one statement, Jesus erased the entire religious tradition of earning God's favor. Jesus said, "Don't you see? Unless you are conceived by God's spirit, you are not God's child." What a shock that must have been! Nothing that I can do will change who my father is. No effort on my part will undo the bloodline I inherited at conception. I am who I am as a direct result of the generating act of my father. And God tells me the same thing. I cannot be like Him unless He generates me. No amount of religious ritual, piety, pleadings, sacrifice, or charity will give me His family resemblance. I can be part of the family only if the Father generates me into the family.

Comments and Reflections:
A surrendered heart brings you into an active family relationship with the Father, the Son, and the Holy Spirit. Leading like Jesus is displaying to others the traits and leadership point of view of your inherited eternal family as an act of service.

---

 relax

LETTING THE WORDS OF JESUS CHANGE ME TODAY

What leadership characteristics do I demonstrate that show I am His child?

How might others react if I were a better example of my Father?

What parts of my life might not reflect my Father's family image?

Who Is Your Father?

*. . . unless one is born **again**, he cannot see the kingdom of God.*
John 3:3

Again—For the second time we must ask the question, "Who is your father?" Jesus tells Nicodemus that this "generating process" is not anything like the world's view of a father's role in conception. It is a generation from above. It is an entirely new thing, unrelated to any physical process. Only God can accomplish it.

The typical "born again" vocabulary of modern Christianity does not quite capture the deeper meaning of Jesus' statement. "Born again" theology tends to emphasize the role of the conceived child rather than the conceiving father. We are exhorted to walk down the aisle or raise the hand or fill out a card or say a ritual prayer in order to make this extraordinary event occur. This is not the focal point of Jesus' teaching.

The Greek word is for again is *anothen*. In every occurrence in the gospel it means "from above." There is no doubt that Jesus pointed toward a new beginning, initiated by an act of God. Sin cannot be cleaned up or erased. It has to be utterly removed. That happens only when the sinner is regenerated as a new person in Christ. Jesus is telling Nicodemus that God has the active role in this process. It is God's regeneration, not ours. No possible child ever says to its potential parents, "Now get out there and get to work so that I can be born." Conception and birth are not decisions on the part of the child. They are the work of the parents. Jesus is laying the emphasis on God and His role.

Does that mean that there is nothing I can do at all? Am I just as much a by-product of someone else in the spiritual realm as I was in the physical world? These questions are both aimed in the wrong direction. First, not a single one of us is simply an accidental by-product. God's plan included our physical birth. We are here on purpose. And secondly, there is something very important for us to do when it comes to regeneration. We are called to repent and turn to God's mercy. We cannot bring about regeneration, but we can certainly desire it. Without repentance, there is no conception.

Comments and Reflections:
If on a scale of 1 to 100, God is perfection and gets 100, an axe murderer would probably score a 5 and Mother Theresa a 95. Colleague Bob Buford suggested to us that Jesus came to make up the difference between whatever our score is and 100 if we repent and accept God's grace. Leading like Jesus starts with honoring this spiritual relationship with obedience.

෩෨

LETTING THE WORDS OF JESUS CHANGE ME TODAY

How do my actions today show thanksgiving to Him?

What else can I do as a leader of others to demonstrate God grace toward me?

What do I need to say to Him in prayer today?

The Power of Us

*Permit it at this time; for in this way it is fitting
for **us** to fulfill all righteousness.*
Matthew 3:15

Us—Rick Warren said in his book, *The Purpose Driven Life,*
"It's not about you." Jesus said on His first day, "It's about
us." Did you realize that Jesus opens His ministry with a
statement about community? He did not say that it was
appropriate *for Him* to fulfill God's plan. He said it was
necessary *for us.* Jesus immediately identifies Himself with
the rest of humanity by including John. The Greek word
hemin is the *inclusive* word. In this tiny Greek word, Jesus
changes everything about the relationship between God and
man.

One of the greatest themes of the New Testament is *us.* Over
and over we are reminded about what God has done for us,
how Jesus is related to us, why the Body is for us. Being a
follower of Jesus is a commitment to *us.* It is never a
rationale for exclusion of others. What the death of Jesus
demonstrated was God's complete identification and inclu-
sion with all of us.

How difficult it is for us to follow Jesus' footsteps here! Man
in opposition to God is man characterized by *exclusion.*
There is always some human rationale for pushing others
away. Race, color, creed, shape, status, power, place, position, language, style, the list goes on and on. And let's not
forget religion. Christianity has become a splintered and
fractured gem of exclusion—every group defying every
other. What has happened to the Lord's words, "that they
may be one"?

If we are going to follow Jesus, we will have to begin with an examination of our fences. Who are we keeping out? Who do we identify as the "others"? Perhaps we need to stand in the waters of the Jordan and hear Him say, "It's about *us*."

Comments and Reflections:
Leadership is not something you do to people; it is something you do with people. When you first realize that leadership isn't all about you, you have started the journey to leading like Jesus. Your next leadership moment will give you a great opportunity to see how far along on the journey you have traveled.

ഇൠ

LETTING THE WORDS OF JESUS CHANGE ME TODAY

How do my actions as a leader clearly include others?

How do I score on the "it's not about me" scale?

What fences do I have that keep me separated from others?

Where do I need God to erase "exclusion" from my life?

Show and Tell

A pupil is not above his teacher; but everyone,
*after he has been **fully trained**, will be like his teacher.*
Luke 6:40

Fully trained—How many training sessions have you attended? How many courses in school, lessons in church, lectures, and seminars have you gone to? How many times have you gone away thinking, "What was that all about?" or "What purpose did that serve?" A onetime class, a once heard sermon, or one course doesn't do much to make us perfectly adjusted to serve our destiny. Jesus had a different approach to training. It was called discipleship. It meant pouring His life into the lives of twelve other men, every day for three years. It was the "living, eating, sleeping, walking, talking, watch how I do things" training. And at the end of those three years, Jesus said, "I have given you everything that you need to know. Now you go out and do what I did."

Few of us take on this kind of training responsibility. We would rather send our people to a short course in business success or sales strategies. But the real purpose of training is to do what Jesus did—to lead someone else in the way of the Master. Training is making a commitment to pour your life into someone else's life.

The idea behind this Greek word, *katertismenos*, is to be shaped so that you are completely adjusted and fit for a purpose. When Jesus trains us, it is always for His purposes and our benefit.

Did you notice that Jesus said, "after he has been *fully trained*"? The real goal of training is to alter life. It is an activity of *mutual* commitment—teacher and pupil. Jesus came from an oriental culture where the bond between master and pupil was much more than course work. It was life work.

In order to lead like Jesus, you must be in training yourself. It is training that will last a lifetime. But others can follow in your footsteps only if you are following in His. Make a commitment to become *fully trained*. Then you will be a perfect fit.

Comments and Reflections:
Rarely do we work exclusively with fully trained and qualified people. Leading like Jesus means a personal investment in the development and qualifying of your people. Remember, Jesus spent most of His limited leadership time on earth training and transforming unlikely people and qualifying them do extraordinary things. A key indicator of your leadership legacy will be how much time and effort you spent on making sure your people receive what they need to be fully trained and qualified.

LETTING THE WORDS OF JESUS CHANGE ME TODAY

What steps am I taking as a leader to help others become fully trained?

What steps do I take that help me become fully trained?

Is my leadership about directing or about transforming?

The Bottom Line

*. . . for apart from Me you can do **nothing.***
John 15:5

Nothing—The Greek word *oudeis* literally means "not one thing." Jesus is speaking to His disciples. He tells them that He is the vital energy of their lives (the vine). They are the recipients of that vital energy (the branches). What they accomplish in life (the fruit) is only accomplished because of the connection they have to Him. Then He says, "If you are not connected to me, you can't do one single thing".

The paradox in this verse is that *everything* is ultimately under Jesus' power. John makes it clear that "not one single thing" was brought into being without Christ's direct involvement. Since this is true for all things, Jesus only points out what should have been crystal clear for His disciples: not one single thing will be done without their total reliance on Him. They are to act explicitly on the foundation that is implicit in creation. They are not to live in a fog about who is behind it all.

There is a personal paradox here too. It is the paradox of a believer like you and me acting in ways that support the false belief that we have to take care of some things on our own. It is the false belief that God leaves the little things up to us while He takes care of cosmic issues. This word shouts a resounding "NO!" Not one single thing gets done unless Christ is behind it. This is an indictment against us every time we think, "I have to do this by myself." For the servant leader, there is no such thing as "doing it by myself." Unless you are connected, "not a single thing" will get done.

Comments and Reflections:
This statement contains a hidden paradox. Look around you. Everywhere people are accomplishing tasks. It doesn't

seem to make any difference if they are connected to Christ. Nonbelievers create great empires, become famous, are wealthy, do amazing works for charity, and give their lives to causes. It is obvious that they are able to do all sorts of things. So, why does Jesus say that apart from His vital energy, not a single thing can be done? Because God has the final word on the eternal bottom line results. He determines if all our striving can make a difference that lasts. An attempted "do it yourself" project is not going to have any eternal value. Remember, as followers of Jesus we are longing to hear these words from our Master, "Well done." What you will hear depends on how closely connected you stayed with Him and how willingly you were to "Invite God in."

&ᘛᘚ&

LETTING THE WORDS OF JESUS CHANGE ME TODAY

Have I been trying to control areas of my life without God's vital energy?

What things do I think I have to do by myself?

What control issues do I need to turn over completely to Him?

All in the Family

*If you **abide** in Me, and My words **abide** in you,*
ask whatever you wish, and it shall be done for you.
John 15:7

Abide—Read the verse carefully. The thought changes from the first "abide" to the second "abide." We would have expected "and I abide in you." But that is not what Jesus says. He says that His *words* abide in me. This Greek word means "spoken words." If you and I are going to lead like Jesus, we need to let what He said permeate us. We need to abide in His spoken commands and teaching.

The Greek word used here is *meinete*. It can be translated as remain, persevere, stay, continue, or abide. It occurs forty times in the Gospel of John. The word borrows a context from the Old Testament where God is portrayed as consistently faithful and steadfast in His commitment to men. God's faithfulness is made evident in sending His Son as the redeemer.

In John's gospel, the idea is expanded to indicate the closest possible relationship between God the Father and the Son. This verse extends this same relationship to those who believe in Jesus as the Christ. In other words, the same harmony and fellowship that Jesus experienced with the Father is offered to Jesus' followers. This unity of wills is the basis for the promise offered in the verse. Saint Augustine said, "Love God and do as you please." The key is to love God, for if we truly love God, what we are pleased to do is His will, not ours.

Every leader knows that personal communication is the fabric of loyalty and trust. But everything said will be of no use at all unless the follower is listening. Jesus expects every follower to listen to Him. You cannot abide without hearing. You can't speak His words to those who follow you unless you hear them from Him. If you're not listening, you're disconnected.

Comments and Reflections:
One of the challenges of leading like Jesus is the intimacy that it requires. Before we can be like Jesus in the way we lead or begin to serve His purpose for our lives, we need to know Him, not just know about Him. It requires pursuing an ongoing intimate relationship with Him through prayer, study of His word, and time alone with Him. Intimacy with Jesus will slow your pace to a walk, expand the power of a quiet moment, calm your anxious striving, and bring peace through you into your relationships. Take a moment to think about what you can do to stick closer to Jesus.

৪৩৫৪

LETTING THE WORDS OF JESUS CHANGE ME TODAY

What am I doing to actively encourage Jesus' words to abide in me?

What could I do today to stick closer to Jesus?

How would this intimacy transform my leadership today?

All Inclusive

*This I command you, that you love **one another**.*
John 15:17

One another—"Playing favorites" is a game that we all know. We learned it as children when we had our special friends, our own clique, or our gang. We used that game over and over to make our way through the work world, picking out those friends who could give us something in return. But this game is of no value at all in Jesus' kingdom. His leadership calls us to put aside our divisions and make all His followers the objects of our efforts to serve. It doesn't matter what role they play. Janitor, receptionist, manager, CEO, teacher, pupil, child, mother, wife, clerk—no position or occupation is outside the scope of *one another*.

There is something special in the grammar of this pronoun. It is plural and an object, not singular and a subject. This Greek word *allelon* means "one another." It is an outward action. It helps us see that servant leadership is about community. "One another" is an outward action.

Consider for a moment the implications of this tiny grammatical fact. Jesus' leadership shows us that love always extends itself to others. *It doesn't matter how our efforts to serve are received.* Embraced or rejected, the call is the same. Loving others is the objective of your life.

Love is never an action that focuses attention on the subject. It is always moving outward toward another person. And love is never exclusive. It is always aimed at *all* others.

Transforming your motivations and intentions into a servant leader will require reevaluation of every aspect of your thinking and behavior. This is not optional. Jesus does not make a suggestion or offer a self-improvement tip. He *commands* it. If you are going to follow Him, you must become one who loves others. In order to do that, you must begin by making Him the object of your love and letting Him become the source and power of your very being.

Think about your direction. Is it outward toward others or inward toward you? Is it singular or plural? Time to decide.

Comments and Reflections:
Unconditional love has the element of loving regardless of how unlovable a person or group of people may be. A key to understanding what goes on when you seek to love unconditionally is to contemplate Jesus on the cross. Whether you are looking at the face in your bathroom mirror or at someone who betrays or disappoints you, you are looking at the object of God's affection and the one who He calls you to treat accordingly.

―――――― ❧ ――――――

LETTING THE WORDS OF JESUS CHANGE ME TODAY

What can I do today to demonstrate the love of Jesus toward those I influence?

How does my life reflect Jesus' command to love?

Have I confused the command to love and the response I expect?

All or Nothing

*If I do not wash you, you have no part **with** Me.*
John 13:8

With—Are you really with it? Or are you just hanging around?

There are several Greek words that could be translated by the English word "with." If we don't understand the difference between these Greek words, we might think that they mean the same thing. But the nuances are important. In the gospel of John, the preposition *meta* takes on the meaning of "being along the way with" or "being in the company with." When Paul uses another preposition that also means "with," *syn*, it has a different sense. It is the "with" of being completely identified with Christ.

Think of the impact John's use of *meta* could have in your work environment. If you are going to be *meta*, you will need to be an active, participating part of the whole. You can't sit on the sidelines and coach others. You will have to get into the game with them. You will need to be part of the company of their fellowship. And Jesus tells us that in order to be a *meta* participant, you must first embrace personal humility. Humility is the hallmark of group identification. It's impossible to be a player-coach if you think you have all the answers. *Meta* leaders are part of the company they keep.

We have all experienced those who are in the group but are not really part of the group. They are with us but they really aren't there. They have their own agenda, their own rules, and their own objectives. A servant leader cannot operate on this basis. A servant leader must jump into the midst, be among, be in the company of, and become a dynamic part of the group. We have an idiom that expresses the need: "Are you with me?" A servant leader has a quick and ready answer: "Yes, count me *in*! I'm part of you."

Jesus made it clear. *Meta* is the preposition of humility. It is the preposition of identity. It is the preposition of fulfilling His calling.

Comments and Reflections:
Jim Collins, reporting his research on leadership in his book *Good to Great*, found humility one of the two key characteristics of great leaders. Two of our favorite definitions of humility are; "People with humility don't think less of themselves, they just think of themselves less" (Norman Vincent Peale) and "People with humility don't deny their power, they just recognize it passes through them not from them" (Fred Smith). Humility is a key heart attitude that keeps us from *edging God out* and putting ourselves on the throne of our lives.

— ⅋)ଫ —

LETTING THE WORDS OF JESUS CHANGE ME TODAY

What am I doing right now to be fully involved in the spheres of influence God has given me?

How does my behavior demonstrate to others that I am ready and willing to serve them?

Do others describe me as a person of humility?

God's Perspective

With men it is impossible, but not with God;
for all things are possible with God.
Mark 10:27

With—"I can't see it," said my son. I told him, "Stand over here next to me and look where I am pointing. Then you will see it." Stand close to me and see from my perspective—that is the meaning of this word.

Here the Greek word translated "with" is neither *meta* nor *syn*. It is *para*, and its primary meaning is, "in the proximity of" or "alongside" or "close at hand." Translating this word as "with" actually removes some of the force of the meaning. Jesus is saying that all things are possible when we stand in close proximity to God. He is suggesting that standing close at hand to the true source of power enables us to see impossible things accomplished. It all depends on perspective. If we place our allegiance with men, we will encounter the impossible. But if we stand in God's company, we take on a different perspective—and everything becomes possible.

Yesterday we saw that *meta* meant humbly participating in the company of others. Servant leaders know that identification with others is one of the keys to *leading like Jesus.* Now we see that "with" includes close proximity to God. Servant leaders have one foot in God's circle and the other in the circle of those they serve. They become the bridge of the possible between God's view and man's horizon. A God-perspective requires God-proximity.

Have you ever experienced the wonder that occurs when you allow God to give you His perspective about the task you face? Have you noticed that the very things you thought were impossible obstacles become the avenues of

His glory? And have you also observed that as soon as you step outside the circle of God-proximity, problems become impossible once again?

"With" is the preposition of servant humility—toward those whom we serve and toward the God whom we follow. There is no servant leader without *meta* and *para*. Be a double "with" follower. Stand in the right place.

Comments and Reflections:
Imagine standing next to God and looking at a picture of what you did today, asking Him to point out what was most important to Him. What would you say to Him if He asked: "What did you do about Jesus today? How well did you honor Him in your thoughts, words, and deeds? How did you express His love and faithfulness to you by imitating His servant heart to others? How often did you give Him thanks for your victories and turn over your cares to Him? How obediently did you forgive as you were forgiven? Did you freely extended grace, mercy, and generosity to others without any strings attached?"

ഓരെ

LETTING THE WORDS OF JESUS CHANGE ME TODAY

What behaviors do I exhibit when "impossible" hurdles face me?

What am I doing to adopt God's point of view on my concerns and issues?

How will I answer the question, "How did you honor My Son today?"

Declaring Friends

*No longer do I **call** you slaves, for the slave does not know what his master is doing; but I **have called** you friends*
John 15:15

Call and **have called**—For many years, Jesus was in the company of men who voluntarily placed themselves in the role of *slaves*. He was the Master. They were the pupils. Jesus tells these men that they were slaves because they did not know the plans of the Master. They only followed orders. This description often fits our own relationship with God. He seems to have secret purposes. "What is God's purpose in this situation?" How many times have you heard a fellow Christian say, "God has His reasons"? Of course, what is implied in such a response is that we mere mortals don't have a clue about what is going on.

Now Jesus changes the status of His followers from slaves to friends. We need to take a very close look at this change. Jesus says that He no longer calls His followers slaves. The first verb for *call* is in the present tense. This implies two conditions. The first implication is that up to this moment, it was appropriate to call these men slaves. The second implication is that as of this moment, their status has changed. From now on, their moment-to-moment relationship with the Lord will be as friends.

Jesus continues. "But I have called you friends" uses a different Greek verb although we translate it with the same English word "call." In the first phrase (I no longer call you slaves), the verb is *lego*. It means, "to speak or say." In this case, Jesus is saying that His followers *are spoken of* as slaves. The word *slave* is attached to them. But the phrase, "I have called you friends" uses the verb *ereo*. This verb means, "to say, declare, and promise." The difference between these two verbs is subtle but important. In the past, the disciples were *spoken of* as slaves but now Jesus is *declaring* them to be friends. The active agent in this change of status is **Jesus**. The change did not occur because these men were suddenly enlightened or because they applied themselves to deeper understanding. Their status is being changed solely because Jesus *declares* them friends.

If a servant leader is following the Master, the time will come when the followers require a change in status. The leader is the one who initiates this change. The disciples did nothing spectacular on this particular day. But Jesus knew it was time for a change. He declared them friends. This declaration required a change in *His* relationship to them. He took the responsibility for the change. He led by becoming what He declared them to be—a friend.

Comments and Reflections:
Leading like Jesus means building trusting relationships through personal example and integrity. It means continuing to foster open communication, honesty, and community by being someone who isn't afraid to speak the truth in love and see beyond people's present level of understanding and competence to what they can become. What barriers remain in your relationships with your people that you can ask God to help you remove?

෨න්ඥ

LETTING THE WORDS OF JESUS CHANGE ME TODAY

What am I doing to transform those who follow me from servants to friends?

What am I doing to prepare those who follow me to take over my leadership?

Have I asked God to prepare my successor?

Come After Me

Follow Me, and I will make you fishers of men.
Matthew 4:19

Follow—But in Greek, it says something a little different. It says, "Come after me."

We looked at the word *come* before. Jesus' entire ministry is an invitation. Here we see that Jesus is really expressing another facet of this ministry. Come after me. But the previous verb for "come" was *erchomai*. Here the adverb is *deute*. It is plural. Jesus calls many. There is an element here that is not easily expressed in English. This is not a stern command. It is *coaching* in its truest sense. It is an expression of tender care and support. It is as if Jesus is saying, "Come on. Don't hesitate. Come along with me and you'll receive something of great value to you."

Deute is modified by the word *opsio*. It means, "behind, in back of, or backwards." This word emphasizes the manner of Jesus' coaching. Come behind me. Put your footsteps in the place where mine have been. Walk in the path I am walking. I am going ahead of you. All you have to do is come along behind me.

Once I took a vacation at a dude ranch in Oregon. We rode horses every day along the mountain trails. Some of those trails were very steep, straddling the edges of sheer cliffs. The guide told us, "Just let the horse find his own way. Don't try to steer him. He knows how to follow the one in front. Don't worry. I'm leading." When we came to the narrowest part, it was hard not to take control. All I could see was the drop-off. But the secret was to let go and let the horse follow in the steps of the one in front. Everyone had to rely on the leader. He knew the path perfectly.

Jesus invites us to come along with Him. But He does not insist that we lead. He asks us only to follow behind. For some of us, learning to follow is a very difficult thing to do. But it is the only safe way.

Comments and Reflections:
To lead like Jesus starts with assuming the role of a servant follower. When you find sureness in your path because of your trust in the One you follow, you can say, "Put your feet in the marks of my steps while I go ahead of you. I'm just following Jesus." Maybe you can only model following in your Master's footsteps rather than proclaim it, but when you do, the trusting will become contagious.

— ∞CR —

LETTING THE WORDS OF JESUS CHANGE ME TODAY

Does my leadership reflect the fact that I am a follower of Jesus?

What am I doing now to insure that I am a "following" leader?

What areas do I need to pray about, asking for God's guidance?

Building an Upside Down Pyramid

I am the good shepherd; the good shepherd
lays down *His life for the sheep.*
John 10:11

Lays down—Have you ever watched a bricklayer? Two things become obvious. Proper foundation and proper order. Without those, the walls come tumbling down.

The Greek verb *tithemi* has a broad umbrella of meanings, all associated with putting something into place. Often the word has the nuance of proper setting, like laying down a foundation or assigning the proper place for a person. Jesus uses the word as a metaphor. The servant leader takes action by offering his life for those in his care. But the metaphor also includes the other meanings of this word. Jesus lays down the foundation needed for His followers. He puts things in their proper order, assigning each to the place of God's choosing. He appoints the proper time, sets the standard, and lays up a heavenly reward. Each of these actions is taken without regard to personal consequences. The focus of the activity is on the need of His followers.

Leaders who follow Jesus have to take two separate and deliberate actions described by this verb. First, servant leaders *lay down* their own lives. They put aside their rights, their agendas, their purposes, and objectives. They lay them on the altar and voluntarily set them in the proper place under God. That is the action of being a servant. It's not *my* agenda that matters. It's not about *me*. But there is another movement required. Once personal concerns have been laid down, another use of *tithemi* is needed. Servant leaders must also lay down the right foundation, the proper assignment, and the right timing *in order that God's calling may be accomplished*. Jesus did not lay down His life for His own purposes. He laid down His life because sacrifice was required in order to fulfill the purposes of His Father. We are called to that same double motion—laying aside ourselves and laying down the necessary elements for others. One without the other is useless.

Comments and Reflections:
Today is the right day to measure your own *tithemi*. Unless you have laid down yourself, you will be of no use to others. Unless you lay down what others need, your denial of self will have no results. Did you lay down twice?

―――――――――――――――――― ℘Ↄ℺ ――――――――――――――――――

LETTING THE WORDS OF JESUS CHANGE ME TODAY

Does my leadership really demonstrate that I am laying down my life for others?

What am I doing to lay the right foundation for those I lead?

Have I put aside my own rights and expectations?

How do my daily actions provide a firm foundation for those I influence?

The Either/ Or Challenge

No one can **serve** *two masters; for either he will hate the one and love the other, or he will hold to one and despise the other.*
Matthew 6:24

Serve—The person who leads like Jesus recognizes one of the fundamental truths about living. Life is all about *whom you serve*. Rick Warren says, "It not about you." Jesus replies, "It's about your master." Jesus invites us to serve Him; to put ourselves in voluntary slavery to the only Master Who actually cares about our well being more than His own life.

We have seen the root of this word before, but it is not what you might think. You might expect that the Greek root would be found in the word "servant" (*diakonos*), but this is not the case. The root word for "serve" is found in *doulos*, the word for slave. The difference is important.

In Jesus' terms, one who serves is not simply an employee. A servant of the Lord is not someone who takes an assignment. The kind of serving the Jesus has in mind is serving under voluntary bondage for life. If you felt a shudder of revulsion when you read those words, you experienced the value that we place on freedom. We all want to be free, by which we mean we don't want to be under anyone else's control. But Jesus sees that such a view of life is an illusion. Life does not include freedom, in spite of the political slogans. Life is being a slave, either to yourself and your desires, passions, and pursuits, or it is being a slave to the Designer of Life. There is no other option. I serve one or the other.

The servant leader has decided to become a slave. To model his Master, the servant leader must bend personal will to the will of the one served. It is bondage of the heart that always results in service with the hands.

Comments and Reflections:
Free will and freedom of choice are not free of consequences. When you choose whom you will serve, you reveal the desires of your heart and what you value most. Who and how you follow will become obvious to others as time goes on.

ഇരു

LETTING THE WORDS OF JESUS CHANGE ME TODAY

How does my daily life demonstrate my complete slavery to Him?

What have I learned about my "freedom" in Christ?

I am in bondage to anything but Jesus?

Follow Through

*And why do you **call** Me, 'Lord, Lord,'
and do not do what I say?*
Luke 6:46

Call—What a mistake we make if we think that this verb is about saying a name! Jesus is revealing an oxymoron in this Greek word, *kaleite*. He is asking a question that completes the thought of being a slave of the master. The slave does not call the name of the master unless he wants the master to come to him. To say, "Lord, Lord" is to call for assistance, to summon someone to your side. No slave would do such a thing unless he was willing to do whatever the master told him to do. It is simply impossible to think that someone who is in voluntary bondage to a master would call the master and then refuse to do what the master says. To refuse is to say, "I never accepted you as my Lord. I do not serve you."

These are harsh words. How many of us have called on Him and then refused to follow. We dishonor the relationship. We reject His sovereignty. If we are going to follow Him, we do what He says.

There is an unusual miracle at the beginning of the Gospel of John. It is the water turned to wine. Look at it again (John chapter 2). You will see something that overshadows the wedding feast. It is the statement of Mary. "Whatever He says, do it." That is the mark of a follower, a servant of the master. John chapter 10 uses the same idea when Jesus says that His sheep hear His voice when He calls them. Calling is not just signaling someone's name. It is verbal declaration of submission and commitment.

If you call Jesus Lord, you are willing to do whatever He says. If you call Him Lord but then refuse to follow His instructions, you are a living oxymoron. Don't call unless you are ready to commit. If you call, do whatever He asks.

Comments and Reflections:
The most effective way to get the Word into your life is to apply it. Think of a portion of God's Word that was especially meaningful to you when you first surrendered to His Lordship. Try living it out in a new way within the next twenty-four hours as a reminder of His faithfulness and grace to you.

ഌൟ

LETTING THE WORDS OF JESUS CHANGE ME TODAY

What part of Scripture did God bring to mind as I thought about my call?

How can I make my call more effective in my life?

What do I need to pray about regarding my submission and obedience?

Don't Miss It

. . . and when He had given thanks, He broke it, and said,
"This is My body, which is for you"
1 Corinthians 11:24

Broken—The missing word. The Greek New Testament is translated from hundreds of fragments. The exact wording of these fragments is not always identical. In this verse, one set of ancient manuscripts includes the word "broken." Another set does not. But it is a word that cannot be ignored even if it is not in some of the earliest manuscripts. In fact, you have probably heard this word repeated many times when you participated in the Eucharist, even though it is not in the oldest texts. It is now part of our ritual of this sacrament.

The Greek root word for "broken" is *klao*. Jesus did not initiate the ritual of breaking bread. In Jewish custom, every meal began with this preparatory step. But Jesus did alter the meaning of this common practice. It would no longer be simply the beginning of a meal. From this point on, it would symbolize the life broken for others.

You may have noticed that this is the first verse that does not come directly from the Gospels. Nevertheless, it comes from the mouth of Jesus. By the time the Lord's Supper became a ritual in the early church, Jesus' purpose on earth had been accomplished. Now the message was being spread everywhere. And with that message, a common practice was transformed into a sacred reminder. Jesus was broken for you.

Leading like Jesus transforms life's simplest actions into sacred offerings of praise.

Comments and Reflections:
Leading like Jesus is not a course; it is a lifestyle. The character of the servant leader is a life broken for others. Every time we eat, we can remember that the broken life is found in the simplest of tasks and the most basic functions of life. Make *klao* your missing word. It is the hidden nature of a broken life that matters most. Eat, and remember.

80C8

LETTING THE WORDS OF JESUS CHANGE ME TODAY

How do the actions of my life demonstrate "brokenness" for others?

Where is God pressing me to be broken in His service?

How can I make the simple tasks of my life "broken bread" for God?

From Beginning to End

Not so with you. Instead, whoever wants to become
great among you must be your servant
Matthew 20:26 NIV

Not—Greek has more than one word that means "not." The first is *me*. The second is *ouk*. The difference between these words is so important that we should have a marginal note in every English translation.

Me is a conditional "not." It is the "not" that is governed by circumstance. For example, "I may *not* be able to do what you ask" is governed by factors that might change. The idea is that a person weighs the consequences to determine whether or not circumstances are in his favor before he decides to act on behalf of another. In the first letter of John we are told that this kind of calculation is *not* love, no matter what the resulting action might be.

This verse uses the other word for "not"—*ouk*. This "not" is absolute. It has no qualifications. It means "never the case." Jesus says that no follower of His will ever calculate the cost of serving before he takes the actions of serving. This is about as strong a statement as you will find. It is simply not possible to say that you know God if your demonstration of love is subject to weighing the conditions. God's love demonstrates itself by giving no matter what the circumstances and conditions. Period!

In Greek, word order is often changed to show emphasis. Here the *first* word (the word of most importance) is *ouk*. The verb follows. Literally, Jesus says, "Not (never) is it so among you." If Jesus thought it was so important, then we better pay attention to this tiny word.

Our entire study began with this verse from Matthew. Now it ends with the same verse. In between is the decision to change your life from *me* to *ouk*. From "we'll see" to "of course." From "it depends" to "no matter what."

Jesus makes it very clear. It's *ouk* about *me*.

Comments and Reflections:
"It's *ouk* about *me*," Jesus of Nazareth.

ഇരു

LETTING THE WORDS OF JESUS CHANGE ME TODAY

What did I learn about conditions that I have placed on my leadership?

What areas of my leadership have been subject to calculating before acting?

Where do I need to reassess my leadership point of view?

Index to Scripture Verses

About the Author

Dr. A. J. Moen ("Skip" to his friends) and his wonderful wife Rosanne live near Orlando. Skip has two bachelor's degrees in education and philosophy, two master's degrees in philosophy and philosophy of religion and a Ph.D. from Oxford University, England, in philosophy and theology. Skip has taught at several universities. He is currently the dean of the Department of Biblical Leadership at Master's Divinity School (http://www.mdivs.edu) and a chair with BBL Forum (http://www.bblforum.com).

For more than twenty years, he provided management consulting services to the telecommunications industry. During that time, he created and operated an independent charity fund-raising program that served more than sixteen thousand grassroots charities. As an entrepreneur, Skip owned several businesses from toy production to salons and spas. He was President of the North American division of a high-tech Internet business headquartered in Hong Kong.

God redirected Skip's life through a life-altering crisis. He began to write about the impact of faith in the aftermath of disaster. He has written more than one hundred articles and several books, many available on his web site (www.atgod-stable.com). Subscribers to the web site receive a daily word study from Greek or Hebrew, revealing the often-overlooked treasures of the Bible.

Skip tells people, "I had everything in life except purpose. God had to take everything away to give me purpose. It was the best trade I ever made." Skip's passion today is to teach others about the depth and power of every word chosen by God.

You can reach Skip at his web site or by e-mail: skipmoen@comcast.net.

A FREE OFFER TO EVERY OWNER

Everyone who purchases *Words to Lead By* can receive Today's Word from At God's Table for FREE for thirty days. Today's Word is a daily e-mail column that teaches the life changing power of a single word from Scripture. You can have this short study delivered to your e-mail address by simply going to this link:

http://www.atgodstable.com/login/special.cgi

Your servant,

Skip Moen

NOTES

NOTES